EP
Earth Science
Printables:
Levels 1-4

This book belongs to:

_____

This book was made for your convenience. It is available for printing from the Easy Peasy All-in-One Homeschool website. It contains all of the printables from Easy Peasy's earth science course. The instructions for each page are found in the online course.

Easy Peasy All-in-One Homeschool is a free online homeschool curriculum providing high quality education for children around the globe. It provides complete courses for preschool through high school graduation. For EP's curriculum visit allinonehomeschool.com.

EP Earth Science Printables: Levels 1-4

ISBN: 9798568655107

First Edition: December 2020

Mapping

On the map below, color the mountain areas brown and the desert areas yellow.

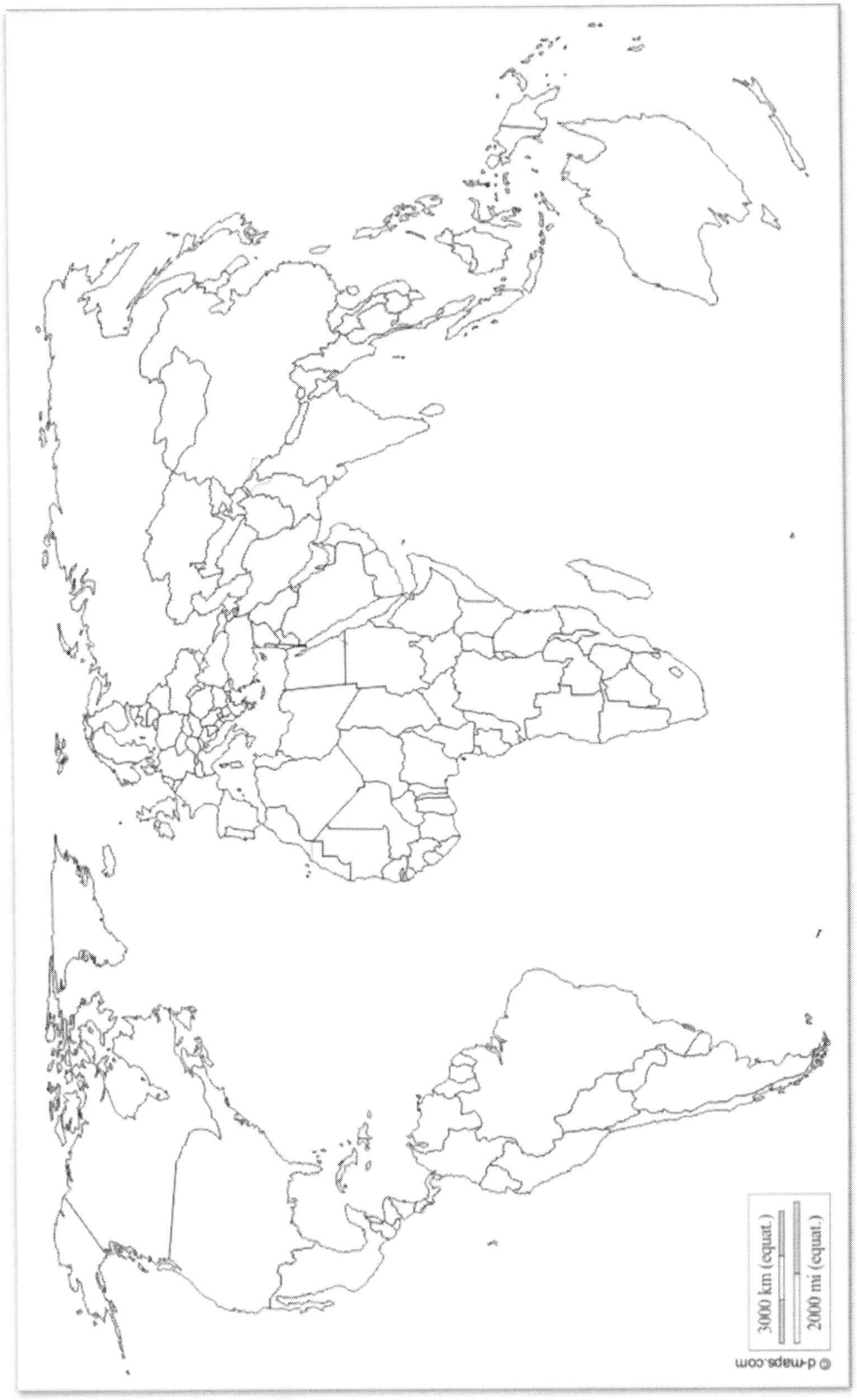

My Rock

Fill in this worksheet on your rock. Draw a picture of it in the box.

Color: _____

Texture: _____

Weight: _____ (heavy/light)

Luster: _____

Hardness: _____

Streak: _____

Cleavage: _____

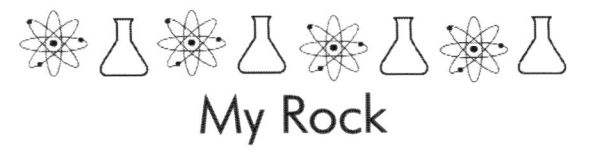

My Rock

Fill in this worksheet on your rock. Draw a picture of it in the box.

Color: _____

Texture: _____

Weight: _____ (heavy/light)

Luster: _____

Hardness: _____

Streak: _____

Cleavage: _____

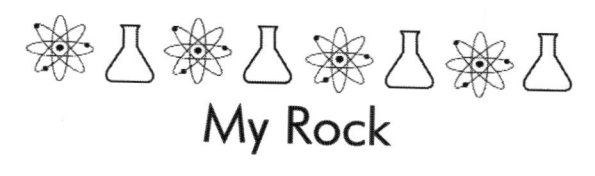

My Rock

Fill in this worksheet on your rock. Draw a picture of it in the box.

Color: _____

Texture: _____

Weight: _____ (heavy/light)

Luster: _____

Hardness: _____

Streak: _____

Cleavage: _____

Water Cycle

Color this picture of the water cycle. Can you describe the cycle using the words in the box?

collection	condensation	evaporation	precipitation

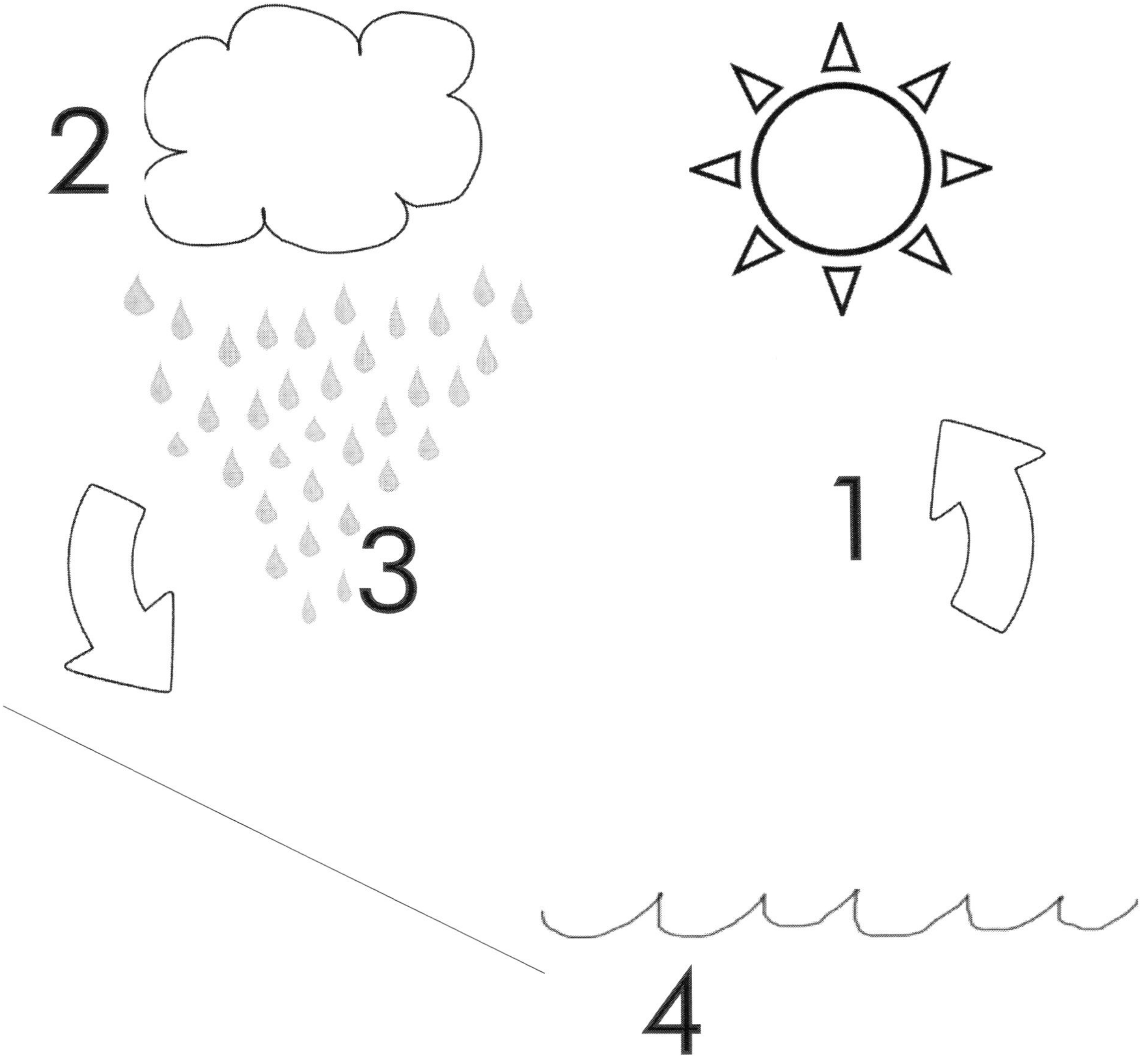

2

3

1

4

1. _____   2. _____

3. _____   4. _____

(This page left intentionally blank)

Cloud Types

Cut out each box and glue to a paper or piece of card stock. Do you see any of these types of clouds outside?

Cirrus

Cumulus

Stratus

Cirrocumulus

(This page left intentionally blank)

Cloud Types

Cut out each box and glue to a paper or piece of card stock. Do you see any of these types of clouds outside?

Stratocumulus	Altostratus
Altocumulus	Cumulonimbus

(This page left intentionally blank)

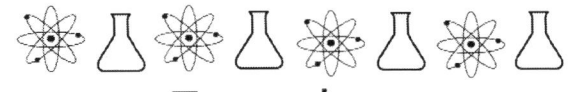

Tornadoes

Circle T for true or F for false for each of the following sentences.

A tornado destroys everything in its path.   T   F

Go into a large room if there is a tornado warning.   T   F

You will always notice a funnel before a tornado strikes.   T   F

The sky may be blue at the time you hear a tornado
watch.   T   F

A tornado can throw cars and trucks into the air.   T   F

A tornado looks like a funnel with the fat part at the top. T   F

There will seldom be lightning during a tornado.   T   F

A tornado may hit your home and leave your neighbor's
home alone.   T   F

When you hear a tornado warning, get in the car and
drive as fast as you can in the opposite direction.   T   F

When a tornado is coming, get out of a car and go
inside a house.   T   F

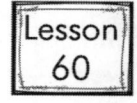

Tornadoes

Use the words from the box to fill in the blanks below.

basement	bathroom	black clouds	ditch	funnel
hail	train	warning	watch	windows

A tornado looks like a _____.

Before a tornado, you will probably see _____.

A tornado can sound like the roar of a _____.

A tornado may also have thunder, lightning, rain, or _____.

A tornado _____ means a tornado may develop later.

A tornado _____ means a tornado has been seen.

Stay away from _____ during a tornado.

The best place to be during a tornado is in a _____.

If you don't have one, the next best place is a _____ or other small room in the center of the house.

If you are outside and see a tornado, go to a _____.

Lightning

Circle T for true or F for false for each of the following sentences.

You usually see lightning before you hear thunder.   T   F

Lightning never strikes the same place twice.   T   F

Someone is struck by lightning every day.   T   F

Seek shelter under a tree if there is lightning.   T   F

Stay away from metal when there is lightning.   T   F

Lightning storms can occur in any season, but are most
common during the spring and summer months.   T   F

During a lightning storm, be sure to call your friends to
make sure they are safe.   T   F

When you see the sky light up, but don't see bolts of
lightning, the storm has passed.   T   F

Always use an umbrella to protect yourself from lightning. T   F

In a storm, stay by the window so you can watch for
lightning strikes.   T   F

Lightning

Use the words from the box to fill in the blanks below.

electricity	fire	lightning	path	phone
shelter	tallest	thunder	tree	water

Lightning and _____ occur together.

Unless there's an emergency, don't use a _____.

Lightning hits the _____ objects.

When lightning strikes, it can start a deadly _____.

Lightning will always take the shortest _____.

When lightning strikes a _____ it can cause an explosion when it heats up the sap.

Stay away from _____ during lightning.

Lightning is _____.

About 100 people die each year due to _____.

Never seek _____ from lightning under a tree.

Hurricanes

Circle T for true or F for false for each of the following sentences.

If a hurricane is in the forecast, flashlights, batteries, and
a radio are good to have.   T   F

Hurricanes usually form over land.   T   F

Hurricanes come up suddenly with little warning.   T   F

Seek shelter under a tree if there is a hurricane.   T   F

The center of a hurricane is called its eye.   T   F

Putting tape on the windows is more effective than
boarding them up.   T   F

Storm surge is an extreme high tide.   T   F

In a big storm, winds can reach over 150 mph.   T   F

A hurricane watch means the storm is within 3 days of
hitting.   T   F

The planes that fly into hurricanes for measurements
of the storm are called Hurricane Hunters.   T   F

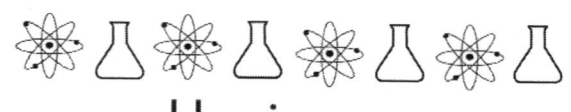

Hurricanes

Use the words from the box to fill in the blanks below.

eye	hundreds	indoors	inland	moving
NOAA	surge	trees	warning	watch

There are over 800 _____ Weather Radio stations to warn you about hurricanes.

A hurricane _____ means the storm is expected to make landfall in the next 2 days.

A hurricane _____ means the storm is expected to strike near you with 73 mph or higher winds.

The wind from hurricanes can blow down _____.

Stay _____ during a hurricane.

The calm center of a hurricane is called the _____.

If you live near the coast, you should head _____.

The air around us is always _____.

Storm _____ can cause tides 25 feet higher than normal!

Flooding can occur _____ of miles from the coast.

Winter Storms

Circle T for true or F for false for each of the following sentences.

A winter storm watch means the storm is coming soon.   T   F

If your car gets stuck in the snow you should leave it.   T   F

Mittens are warmer than gloves.   T   F

Wind chill is the measure of the air temperature.   T   F

Snow storms can happen any time of the year.   T   F

Kitty litter is a good thing to keep in your car in the
winter.   T   F

Turn the lights off if you're stuck in your car at night so
your battery doesn't die.   T   F

If you're trapped in your car, move around as much
as possible to keep yourself warm.   T   F

Keep some bright clothes in your car so if you get
stuck in the snow you can stand beside your car and
be seen.   T   F

Extra blankets should be in your car during the winter.   T   F

Winter Storms

Use the words from the box to fill in the blanks below.

antenna	inside	layers	mouth	poisoning
snowdrift	temperature	warning	watch	winter

Wearing _____ in the winter will keep you warmer.

A winter storm _____ means a cold storm is possible.

A winter storm _____ means a cold storm is on the way.

If your car gets stuck, a bright colored cloth on the car's _____ can help you be seen.

Be sure to crack your car windows while your engine is running to avoid carbon monoxide _____.

Snow storms and blizzards generally occur in _____.

Wind chill is actual _____ combined with wind.

Your car can get stuck in a _____.

Wear a hood that covers your _____.

If at all possible, stay _____.

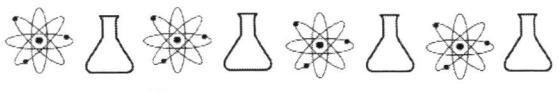

Temperature

Follow the online directions to record the temperature over the next five days.

Date:

Time:

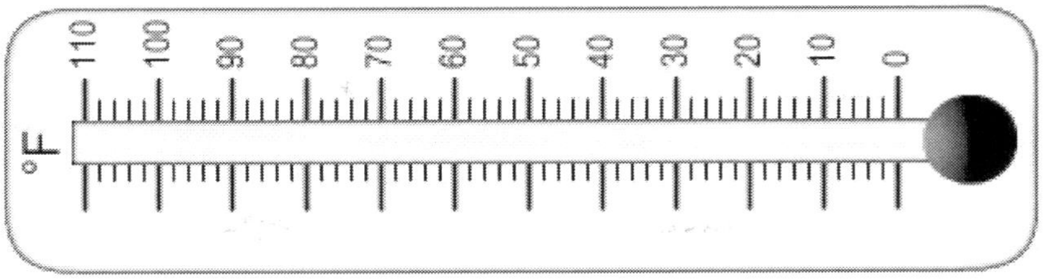

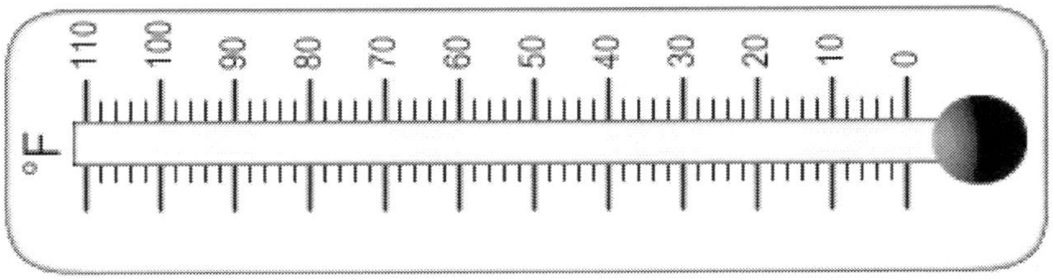

Date:

Time:

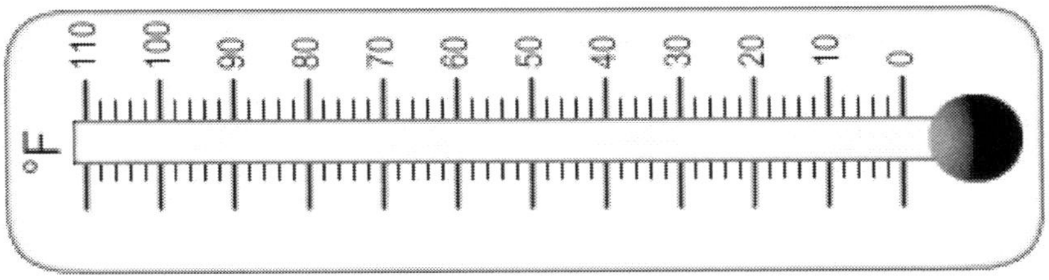

Date:

Time:

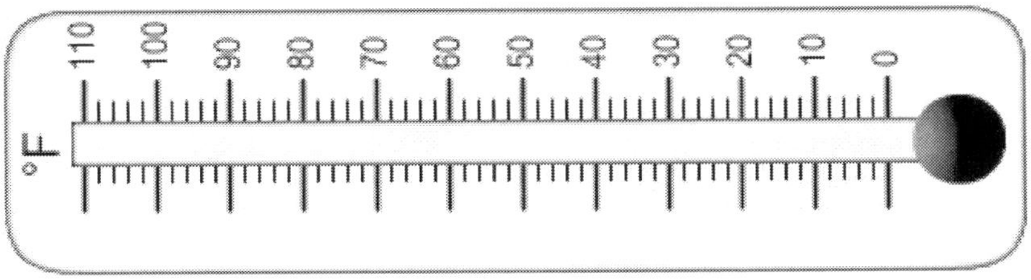

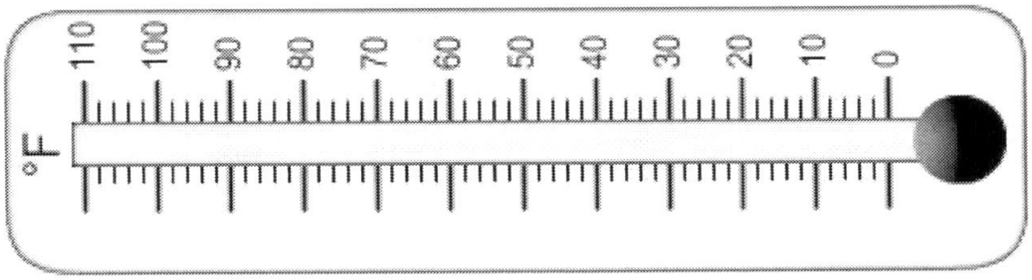

Date:

Time:

Name:

Date:

Time:

(This page left intentionally blank)

Weather Symbols

You can use these symbols to help show the weather conditions for the day while you record the daily temperature. Cut out the symbol or symbols you want to use and glue them to the day's thermometer.

Earth Science
Levels 1-4

(This page left intentionally blank)

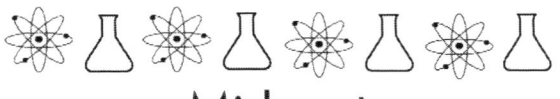

Midwest

Choose the map that contains your state. Follow the directions in the online course to make a weather map.

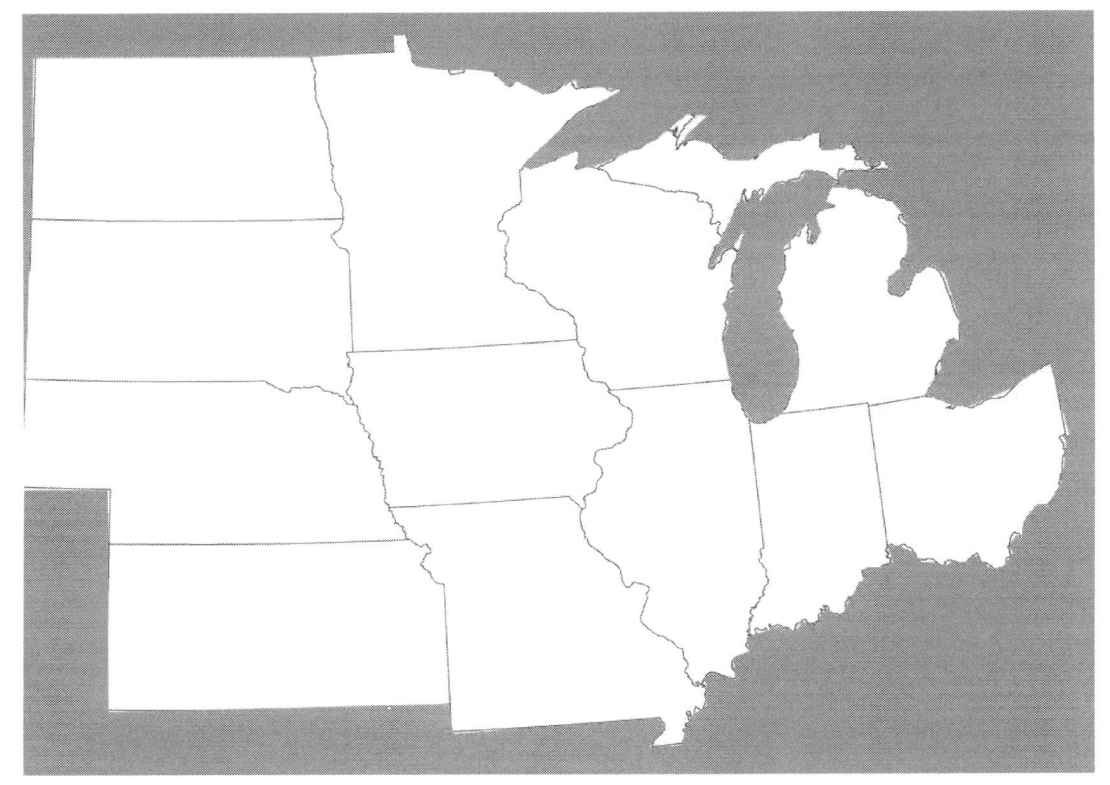

Adapted from: https://freevectormaps.com/united-states/US-EPS-01-1002?ref=atr

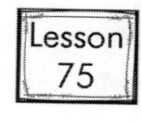
Northeast

Choose the map that contains your state. Follow the directions in the online course to make a weather map.

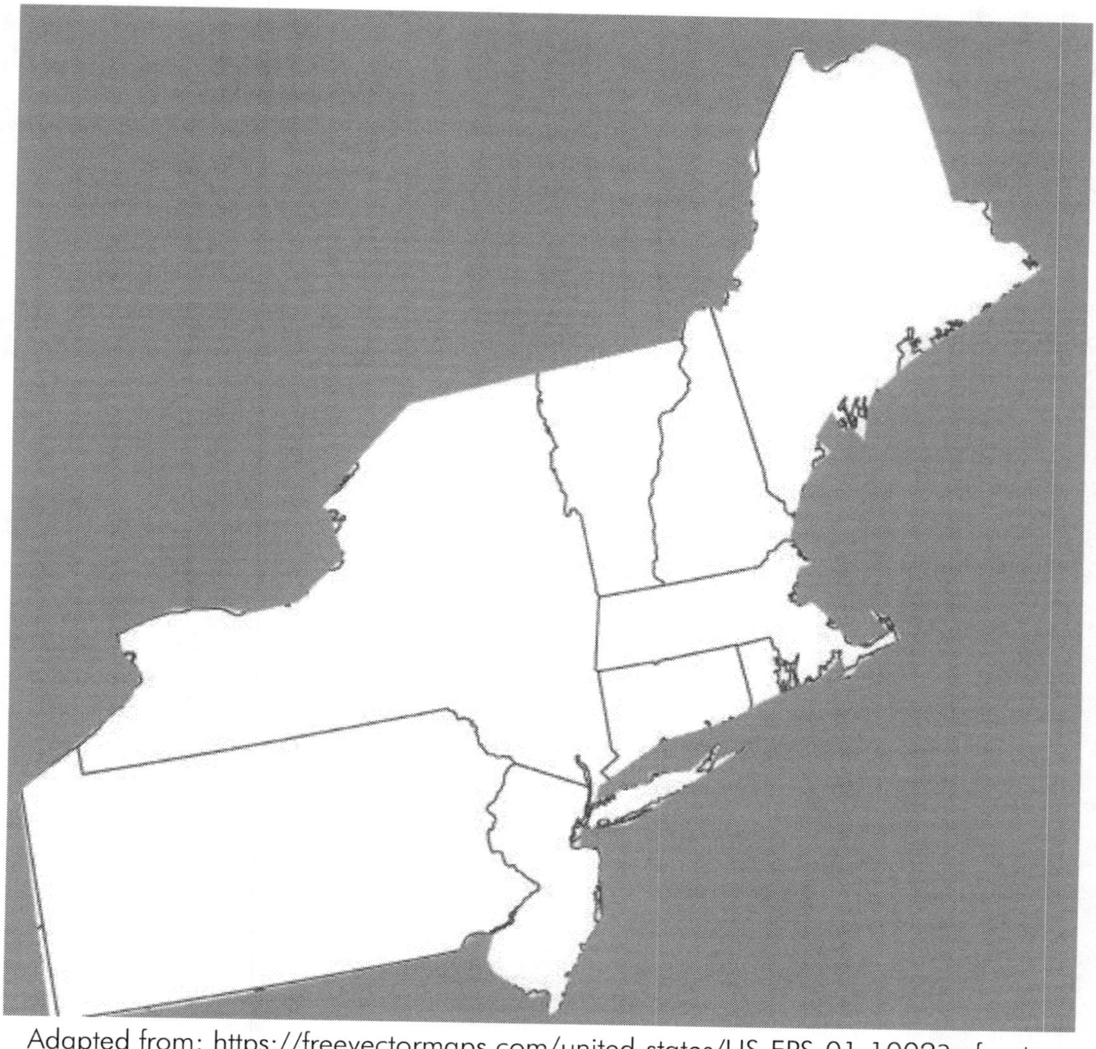

Adapted from: https://freevectormaps.com/united-states/US-EPS-01-1002?ref=atr

South

Choose the map that contains your state. Follow the directions in the online course to make a weather map.

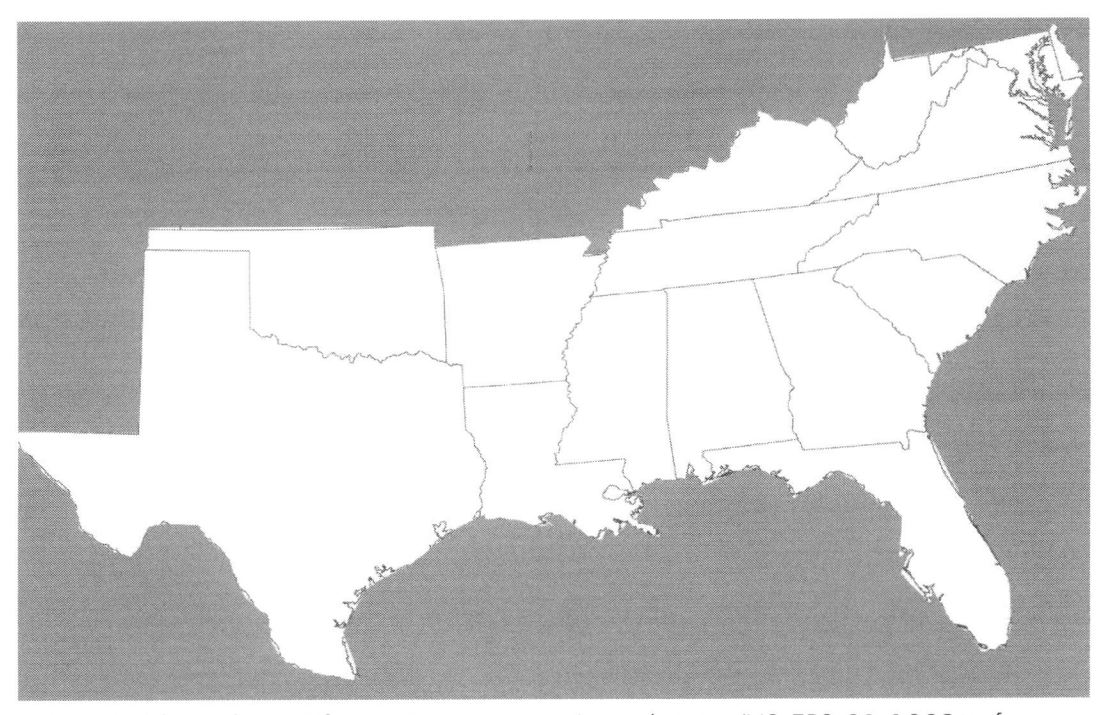

Adapted from: https://freevectormaps.com/united-states/US-EPS-01-1002?ref=atr

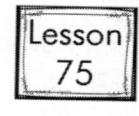

West

Choose the map that contains your state. Follow the directions in the online course to make a weather map.

Adapted from: https://freevectormaps.com/united-states/US-EPS-01-1002?ref=atr

Midwest

Choose the map that contains your state. Follow the directions in the online course to make a weather map.

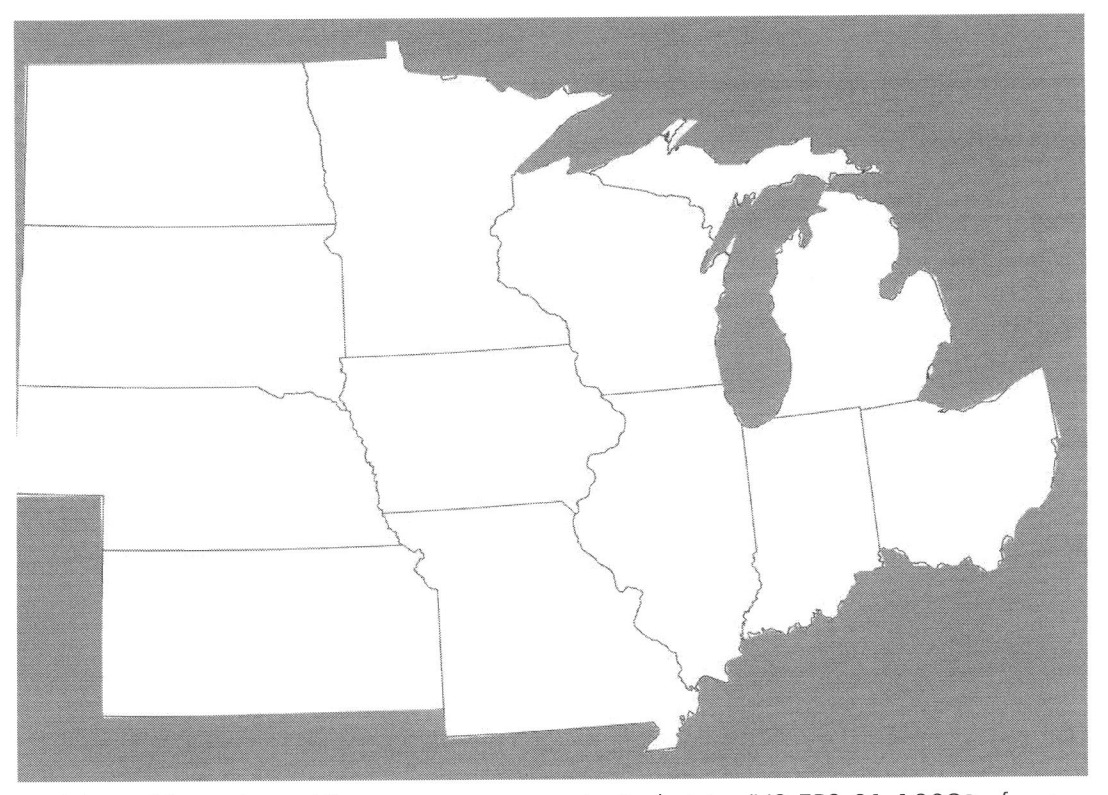

Adapted from: https://freevectormaps.com/united-states/US-EPS-01-1002?ref=atr

Northeast

Choose the map that contains your state. Follow the directions in the online course to make a weather map.

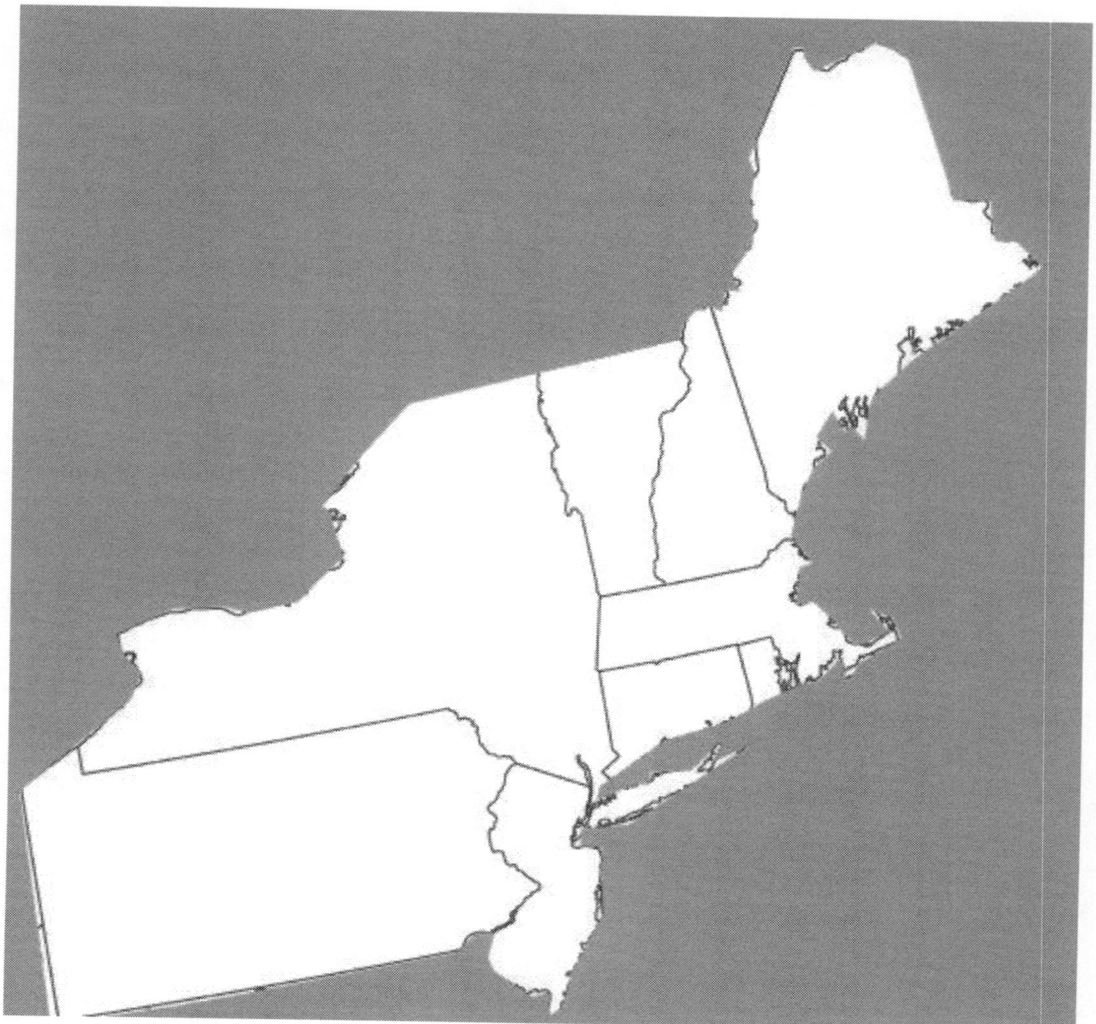

Adapted from: https://freevectormaps.com/united-states/US-EPS-01-1002?ref=atr

South

Choose the map that contains your state. Follow the directions in the online course to make a weather map.

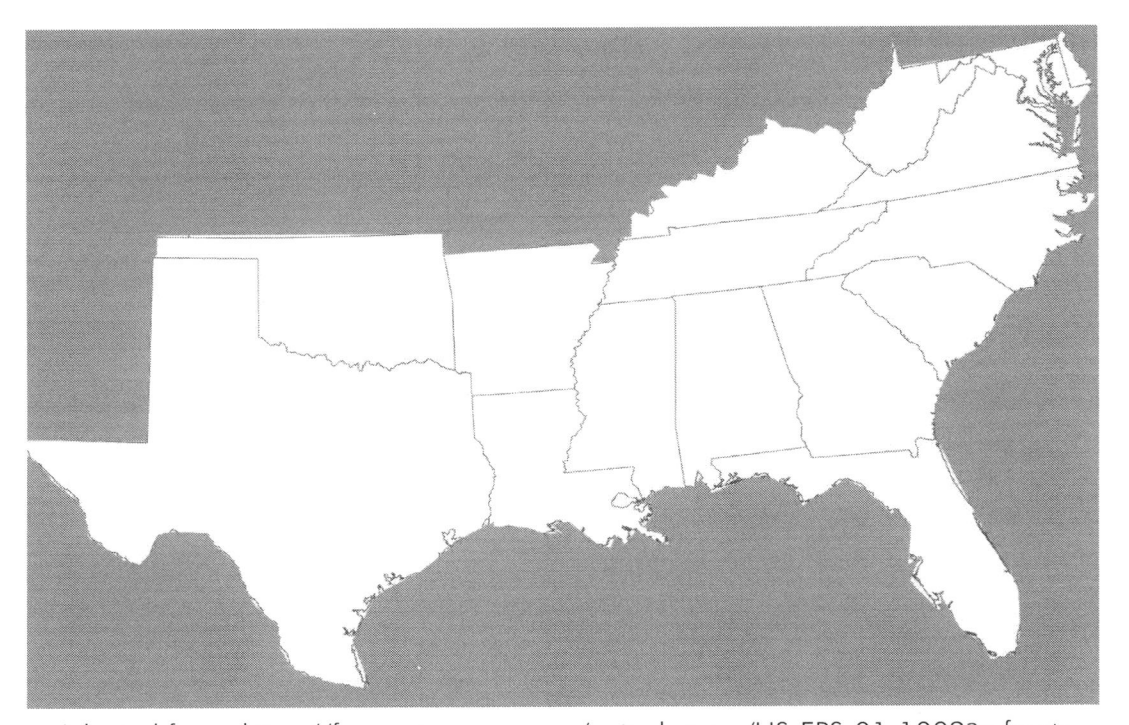

Adapted from: https://freevectormaps.com/united-states/US-EPS-01-1002?ref=atr

West

Choose the map that contains your state. Follow the directions in the online course to make a weather map.

Adapted from: https://freevectormaps.com/united-states/US-EPS-01-1002?ref=atr

Midwest

Choose the map that contains your state. Follow the directions in the online course to make a weather map.

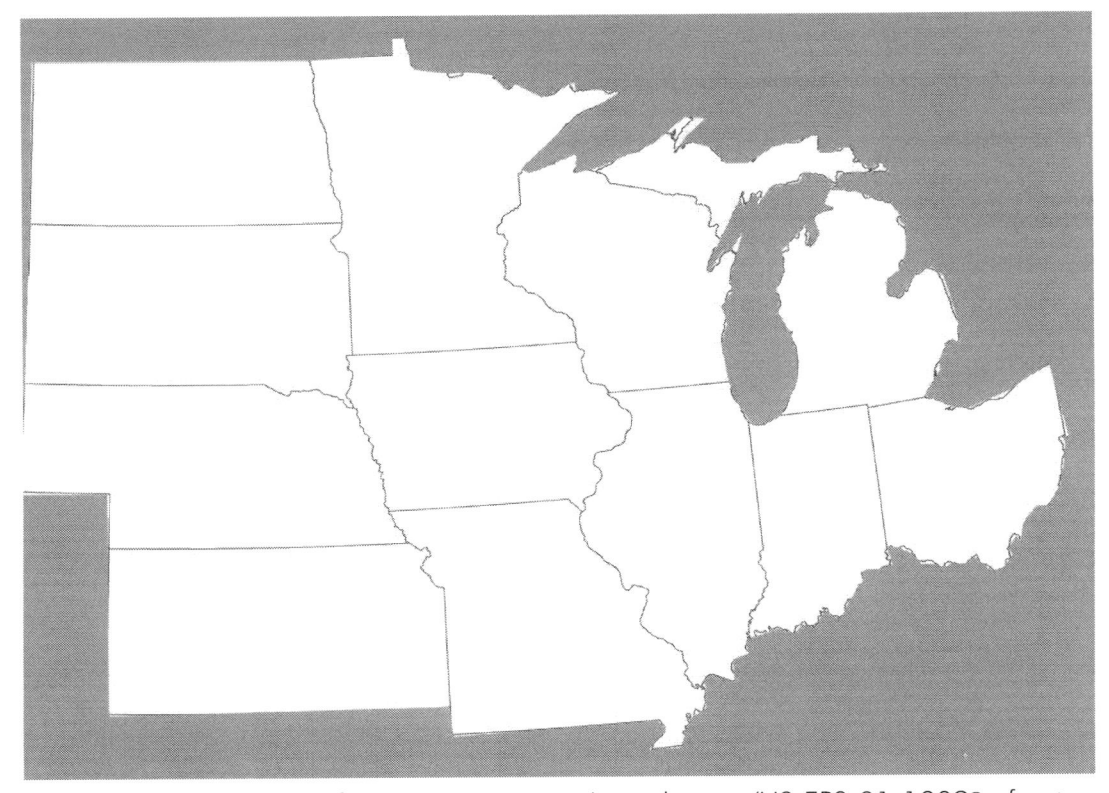

Adapted from: https://freevectormaps.com/united-states/US-EPS-01-1002?ref=atr

Northeast

Choose the map that contains your state. Follow the directions in the online course to make a weather map.

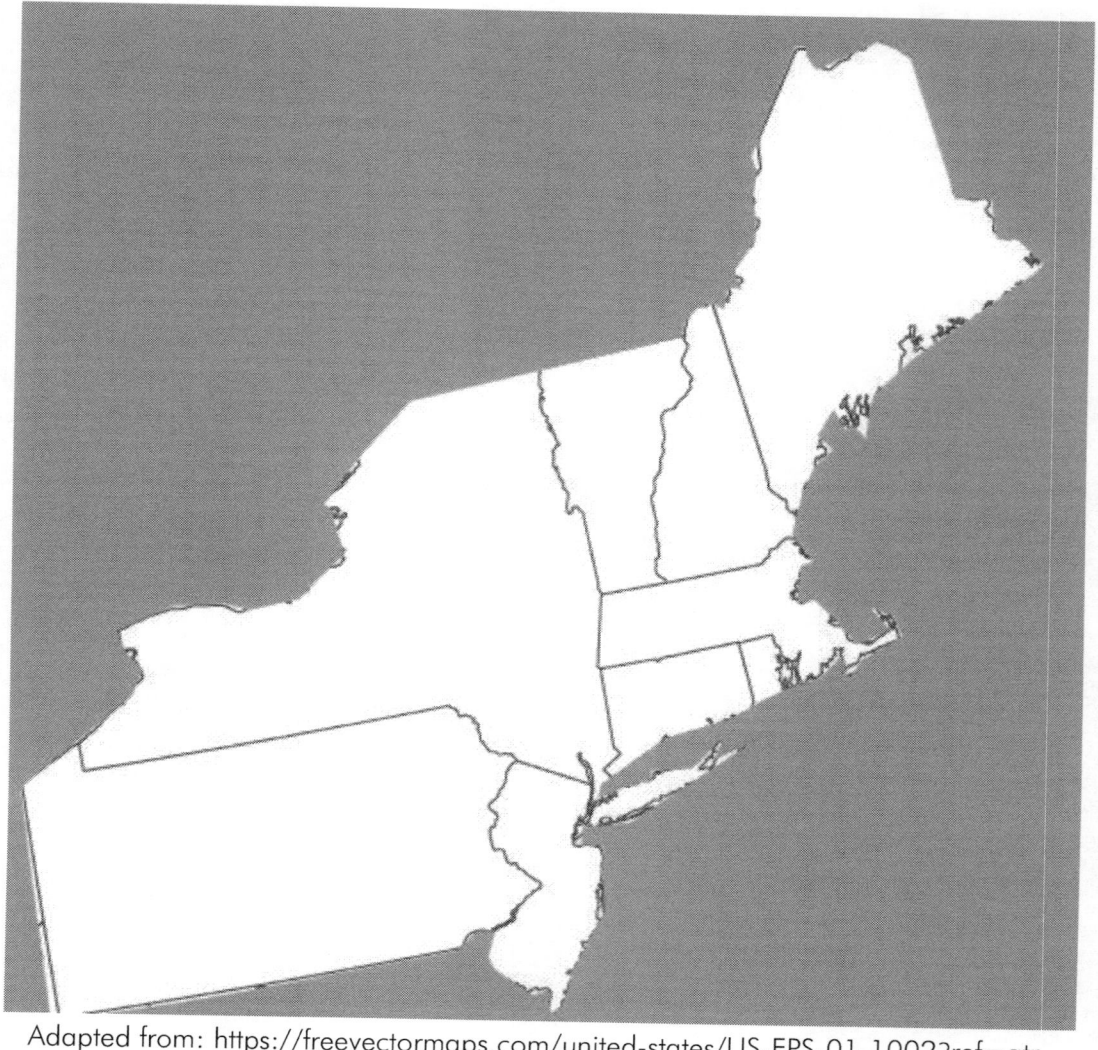

Adapted from: https://freevectormaps.com/united-states/US-EPS-01-1002?ref=atr

South

Choose the map that contains your state. Follow the directions in the online course to make a weather map.

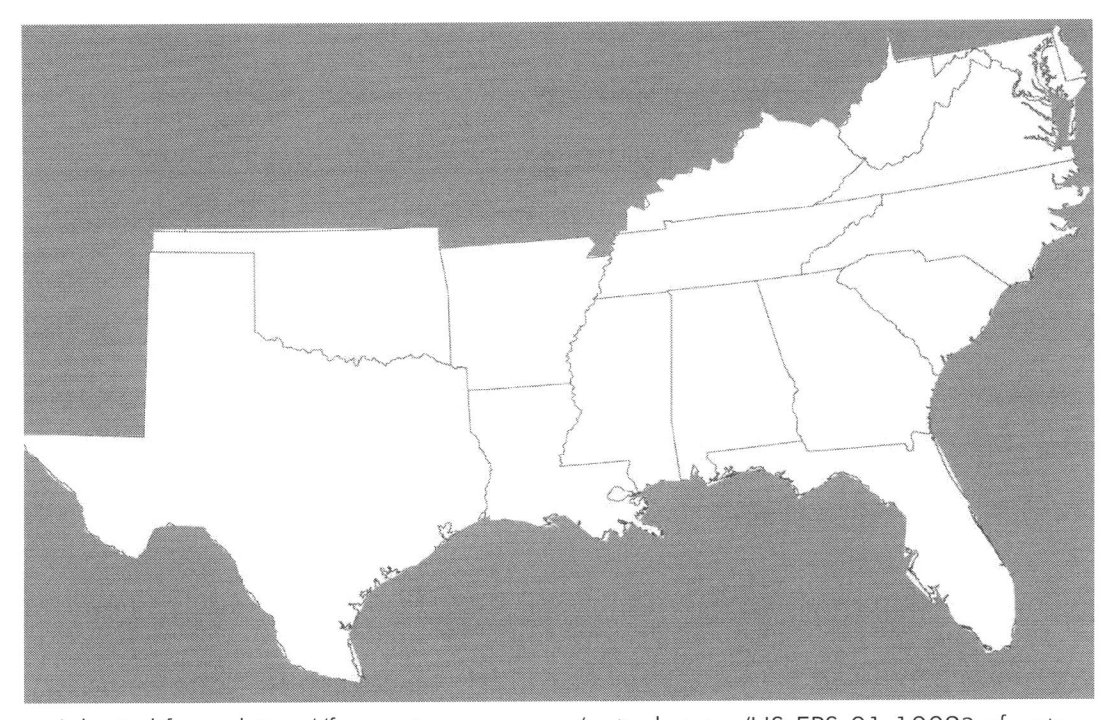

Adapted from: https://freevectormaps.com/united-states/US-EPS-01-1002?ref=atr

West

Choose the map that contains your state. Follow the directions in the online course to make a weather map.

Adapted from: https://freevectormaps.com/united-states/US-EPS-01-1002?ref=atr

Weather Word Search

Find the words from the bottom in the puzzle below. Words can be found any direction, including diagonally.

```
P U W Z P K L B O A E G X U N A H I
O D S T O R M D T R I T X N A C E D
H R S E W R A J U Y M X V P S K B H
I I C K G N A S J R J J L G G S M O
M Z S L R N S I O I N Q N G R A Q T
T Z U O O E Q F N B L I Z Z A R D E
I L T W R U K J I B N S M J K I E M
S E A P B H D E U T S P W Q R X B P
E O F A V Y A L H Q J B V Q O G X E
A P F N L X S G H Q C B J V G F G R
S Z O Z M F I N T O B O I H E A T A
O P R Y O L R M O H Z D L X Z O D T
N O E H Y D I E N W U A G D J M A U
H B C A H A L J E P B N H V Y W G R
U E A I E N Q Q Z H D D E D C E E
G Y S L N R D T G C E F D E O I E H
O S T U P C L N M E G F O G R L Y H
W I N D P O J O Z P Q L U H C L M Z
```

Blizzard	Forecast	Lightning	Storm
Cloud	Freeze	Pressure	Temperature
Cold	Hail	Rain	Thunder
Drizzle	Heat	Season	Tornado
Fog	Hot	Snow	Wind

Mapping

Draw the rivers on the map following the instructions in the online course.

Big Dipper

Find the big dipper in this picture. If you want to, take this page outside tonight and use it to try to find the Big Dipper in the sky.

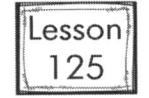

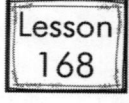

Research Notes

Use these pages to make notes on your topic.

Topic:_____

Resource 1:_____

Info:_____   Info:_____

Info:_____   Info:_____

Info:_____   Info:_____

Resource 2:_____

Info:_____   Info:_____

Info:_____   Info:_____

Info:_____   Info:_____

Resource 3:_____

Info:_____   Info:_____

Info:_____   Info:_____

Info:_____   Info:_____

Resource 4:_____

Info:_____   Info:_____

Info:_____   Info:_____

Info:_____   Info:_____

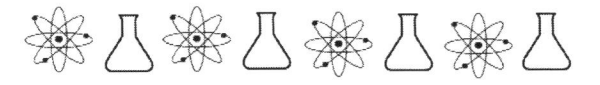
Resource 5:_____

Info:_____   Info:_____

Info:_____   Info:_____

Info:_____   Info:_____

Resource 6:_____

Info:_____   Info:_____

Info:_____   Info:_____

Info:_____   Info:_____

Resource 7:_____

Info:_____   Info:_____

Info:_____   Info:_____

Info:_____   Info:_____

Resource 8:_____

Info:_____   Info:_____

Info:_____   Info:_____

Info:_____   Info:_____

Resource 9:_____

Info:_____   Info:_____

Info:_____   Info:_____

Info:_____   Info:_____

Made in the USA
Columbia, SC
03 September 2024

41562922R00024